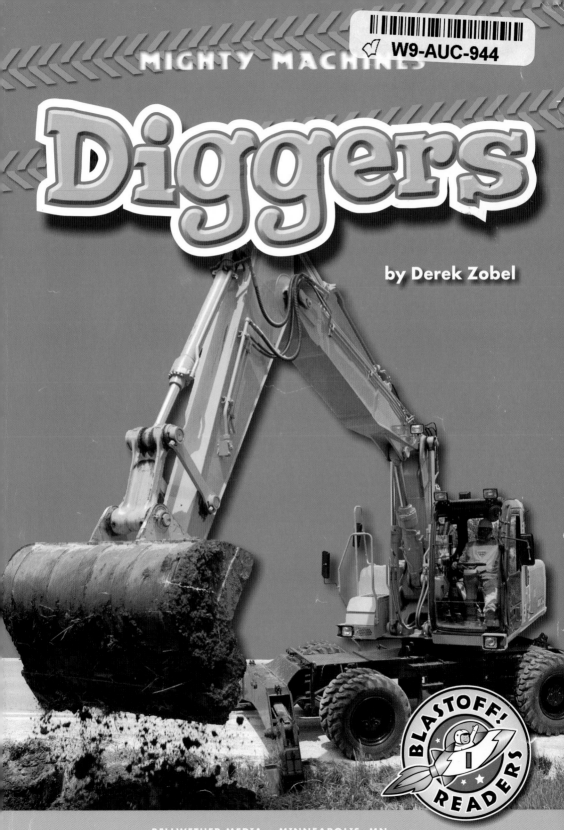

MIGHTY MACHINES

Diggers

by Derek Zobel

BELLWETHER MEDIA · MINNEAPOLIS, MN

Note to Librarians, Teachers, and Parents:

Blastoff! Readers are carefully developed by literacy experts and combine standards-based content with developmentally appropriate text.

Level 1 provides the most support through repetition of high-frequency words, light text, predictable sentence patterns, and strong visual support.

Level 2 offers early readers a bit more challenge through varied simple sentences, increased text load, and less repetition of high-frequency words.

Level 3 advances early-fluent readers toward fluency through increased text and concept load, less reliance on visuals, longer sentences, and more literary language.

Level 4 builds reading stamina by providing more text per page, increased use of punctuation, greater variation in sentence patterns, and increasingly challenging vocabulary.

Level 5 encourages children to move from "learning to read" to "reading to learn" by providing even more text, varied writing styles, and less familiar topics.

Whichever book is right for your reader, Blastoff! Readers are the perfect books to build confidence and encourage a love of reading that will last a lifetime!

This edition first published in 2009 by Bellwether Media, Inc.

No part of this publication may be reproduced in whole or in part without written permission of the publisher. For information regarding permission, write to Bellwether Media, Inc., Attention: Permissions Department, Post Office Box 19349, Minneapolis, MN 55419.

Library of Congress Cataloging-in-Publication Data
Zobel, Derek, 1983–
  Diggers / by Derek Zobel.
    p. cm. – (Blastoff! readers. Mighty machines)
  Includes bibliographical references and index.
  Summary: "Simple text and supportive images introduce young readers to diggers. Intended for students in kindergarten through third grade"–Provided by publisher.
  ISBN-13: 978-1-60014-235-2 (hbk. : alk. paper)
  ISBN-10: 1-60014-235-4 (hbk. : alk. paper)
  1. Excavating machinery–Juvenile literature. I. Title.
  TA732.Z63 2009
  624.1'52–dc22   2008033099

Contents

A digger is a
big machine.
It can dig
big holes.

A digger has a **leg**. The leg keeps the digger steady when it digs.

DEERE

leg

A digger has an arm with two parts. They are the **boom** and the **dipper**.

boom

dipper

DEERE

230C LC

A **bucket** is at the end of the arm. The boom and dipper move the bucket.

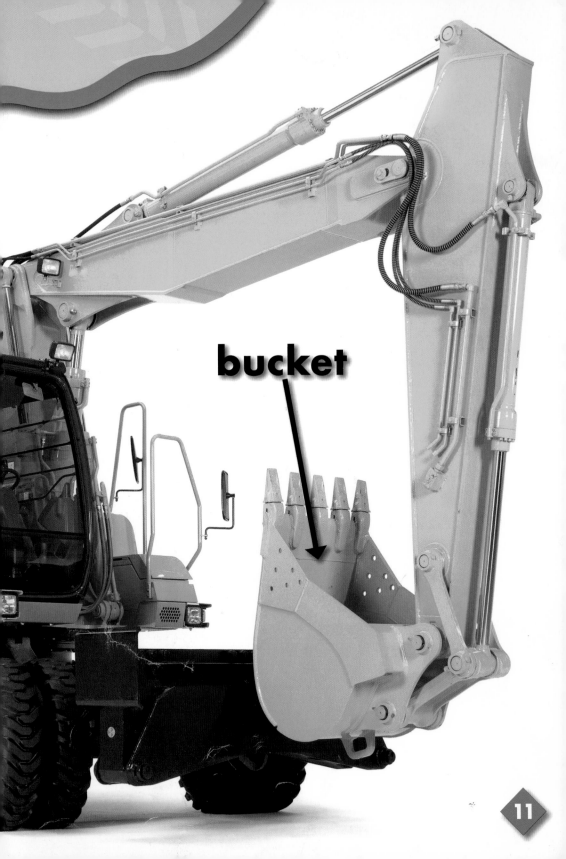

bucket

The bucket digs into the ground.

Some diggers
have wheels.
They work well
on roads.

Some diggers have **tracks**. Tracks grip loose ground well.

tracks

This digger has a **front loader**. It loads dirt into a red **dump truck**.

front loader

A digger can dig a very large hole!

Glossary

boom—part of the arm of a digger; the boom connects to the cab.

bucket—a large scoop at the end of the boom; diggers use the bucket to dig.

dipper—part of the arm of a digger; the dipper connects to the bucket.

dump truck—a large truck that can carry huge loads

front loader—a part of some diggers that can push and carry loads

leg—the part of a digger that keeps it steady when it digs

tracks—a large belt made of metal and rubber; tracks help a digger grip the ground.

To Learn More

AT THE LIBRARY

Eick, Jean. *Diggers*. Eden Prairie, Minn.: Child's World, 1999.

Oxlade, Chris, and Christine Lalla. *This Is My Digger*. North Mankato, Minn.: Sea to Sea Publications, 2007.

Rockwell, Anne. *Good Morning Digger*. London: Puffin, 2007.

ON THE WEB

Learning more about mighty machines is as easy as 1, 2, 3.

1. Go to www.factsurfer.com.

2. Enter "mighty machines" into the search box.

3. Click the "Surf" button and you will see a list of related Web sites.

With factsurfer.com, finding more information is just a click away.

Index

The images in this book are reproduced through the courtesy of Deere, Inc.